DISASTER ZONE

FLOODS

by Vanessa Black

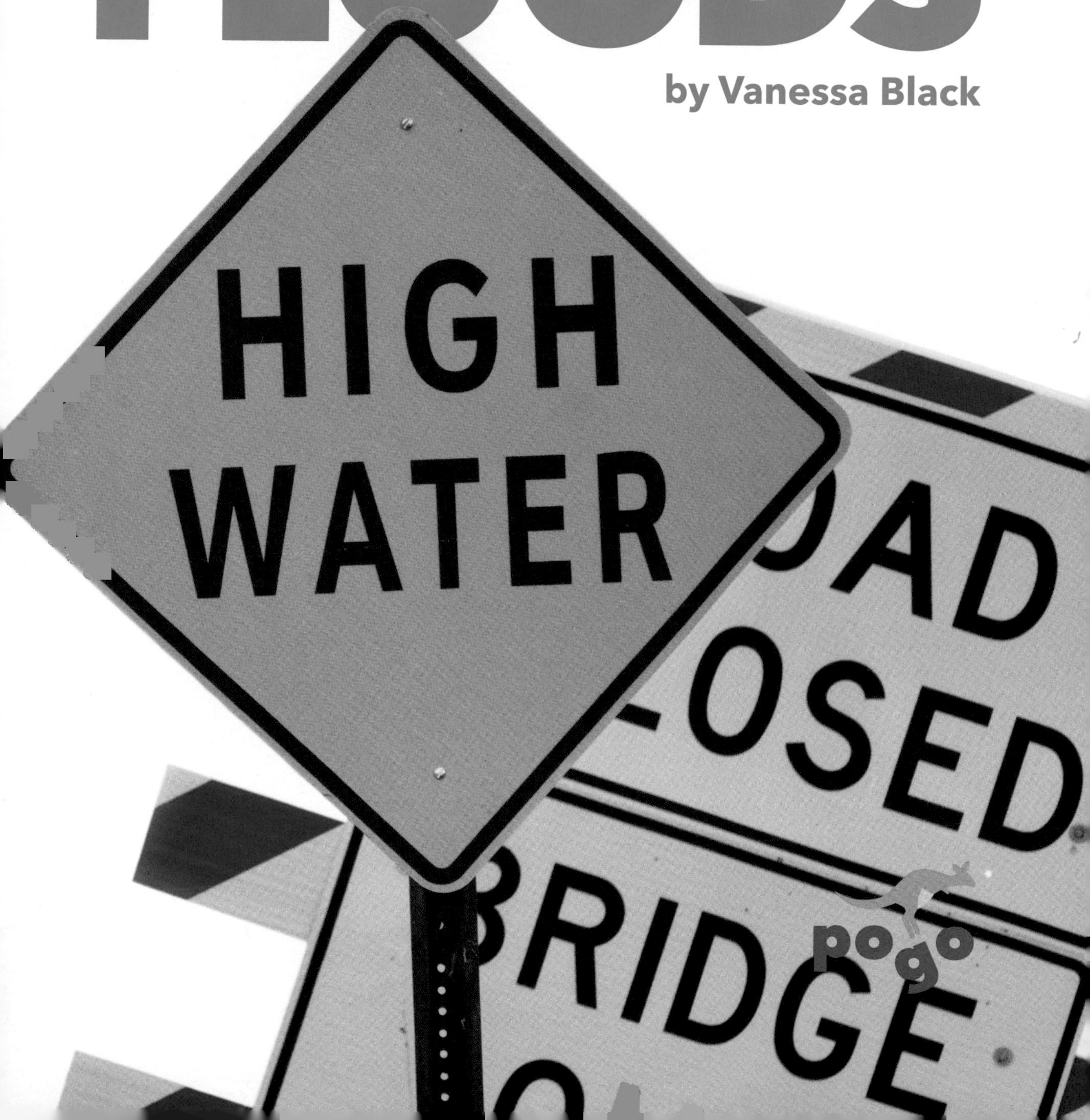

pogo

Ideas for Parents and Teachers

Pogo Books let children practice reading informational text while introducing them to nonfiction features such as headings, labels, sidebars, maps, and diagrams, as well as a table of contents, glossary, and index.

Carefully leveled text with a strong photo match offers early fluent readers the support they need to succeed.

Before Reading

- "Walk" through the book and point out the various nonfiction features. Ask the student what purpose each feature serves.
- Look at the glossary together. Read and discuss the words.

Read the Book

- Have the child read the book independently.
- Invite him or her to list questions that arise from reading.

After Reading

- Discuss the child's questions. Talk about how he or she might find answers to those questions.
- Prompt the child to think more. Ask: Have you ever experienced a flood? Was there any damage?

Pogo Books are published by Jump!
5357 Penn Avenue South
Minneapolis, MN 55419
www.jumplibrary.com

Library of Congress Cataloging-in-Publication Date

Names: Black, Vanessa, author. | Black, Vanessa. Disaster zone.
Title: Floods: disaster zone / by Vanessa Black.
Description: Minneapolis, MN: Jump! Inc. [2017]
Series: Disaster zone
Audience: Ages 7-10. | Includes bibliographical references and index.
Identifiers: LCCN 2016005566 (print)
LCCN 2016006051 (ebook)
ISBN 9781620313985 (hardcover: alk. paper)
ISBN 9781624964459 (ebook)
Subjects: LCSH: Floods–Juvenile literature.
Classification: LCC GB1399.B53 2017 (print)
LCC GB1399 (ebook) | DDC 551.48/9–dc23
LC record available at http://lccn.loc.gov/2016005566

Series Editor: Jenny Fretland VanVoorst
Series Designer: Anna Peterson
Photo Researcher: Anna Peterson

Photo Credits: Alamy, 8-9, 10-11, 14-15, 16-17; Corbis, 18; Getty, 19; iStock, 1, 4, 5, 20-21, 23; Shutterstock, 3, 6-7, 12, 13; Thinkstock, cover.

Printed in the United States of America at Corporate Graphics in North Mankato, Minnesota.

TABLE OF CONTENTS

CHAPTER 1

IT'S A FLOOD!

Imagine you live near a river in Iowa. It is early spring. The air is getting warmer. Snow is melting quickly.

Then, it starts to rain. It rains and rains. Streams fill up fast. They dump into rivers. The rivers get higher and higher.

Soon the rivers can't hold any more. They overflow. It's a flood!

Water floods onto the land. It covers farms. It destroys **crops**.

Water flows into the street. It floods homes. It ruins shops.

WHERE DO THEY HAPPEN?

Most floods happen near rivers or coasts.

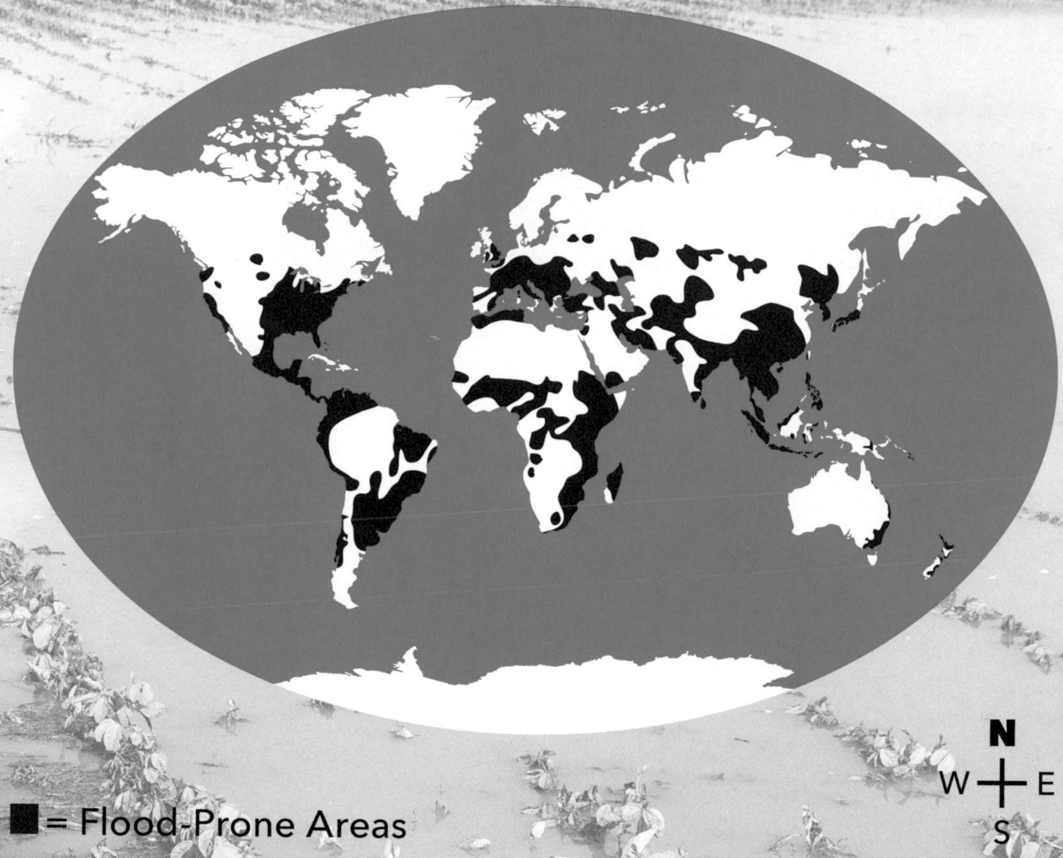

Nearby, another river swells. People hope the **dike** is strong enough to hold the water. But the water is too powerful. The dike breaks.

It's a **flash flood**!

DID YOU KNOW?

A dike is a wall made to prevent rivers or the sea from flooding land.

dike

All floods are dangerous, but flash floods are especially scary. They happen fast. People do not have time to prepare. Water rushes. Cars get carried away. People run to high ground. Some drown.

DID YOU KNOW?

Water is unsafe to drink after a flood. It can carry disease.

CHAPTER 2

DEADLY FLOODS

During **monsoon** season in **Bangladesh**, flooding covers up to two-thirds of the country! People build homes on **stilts**.

They use boats to get places. Kids attend floating schools.

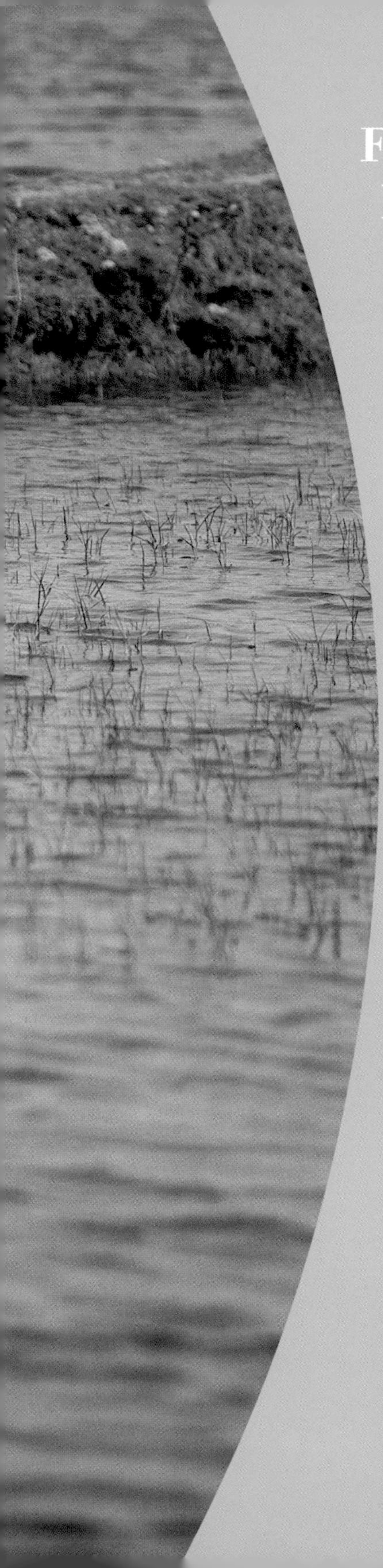

Flooding is a way of life, but it can be deadly.

In 1974, 27,000 people died from flooding in Bangladesh. Many of them drowned. Others were killed by floating **debris**.

That wasn't the end of the problem. The flood killed crops. There was no food. As many as 1.5 million people starved to death.

Sometimes natural disasters, like **hurricanes**, cause floods. In 2005, Hurricane Katrina hit New Orleans, Louisiana. It caused walls of water to **converge** on the city. **Levees** broke. About 80 percent of New Orleans was underwater.

DID YOU KNOW?

When China's Yangtze River flooded in 1931, as many as 3.7 million people died. It remains the highest number of flood-related deaths in history.

CHAPTER 3

STAYING SAFE

The **National Weather Service** issues flood watches and warnings. It is important to listen. If you are told to **evacuate**, you need to go.

Floodwaters are powerful. It only takes six inches (15.2 centimeters) of moving water to knock you off your feet. A car floats in a foot (30 cm) of water. Cars can roll, trapping you inside.

If you live in a flood-prone area, be ready. You can prepare for floods by making sandbag barriers. Place them around your home to help keep water out.

Keep an emergency kit. It should have bottled water, food, a cell phone, and any medications you need.

Be prepared, and you can stay safe in a flood.

sandbags

ACTIVITIES & TOOLS

TRY THIS!

BUILD A DIKE

Build a dike, cause a flood, and see how much – or how little – it takes to create a disaster zone.

What You Need:

- a thick cardboard tube, cut in half lengthwise
- sand
- a hose hooked up to water
- small rocks

1 Dig a long, narrow trench in the sand.

2 Put the cut cardboard tube in the trench. This will be your river.

3 Push the sand up next to the tube so that the sand is level with the top of the cut tube.

4 Make a dike out of the rocks on the sides of the cut tube.

5 Fill the river using the hose.

6 Keep filling the river until it is overflowing.

7 Does the dike hold the water?

GLOSSARY

Bangladesh: A country in Southeast Asia that is prone to flooding.

converge: To move toward a point.

crops: Plants grown for food.

debris: Anything that a flood picks up as it flows along, such as rocks, cars, parts of buildings, wood, or other things.

dike: A long wall used to keep water off of land.

evacuate: To leave a dangerous area.

flash flood: Rapid flooding, usually resulting from heavy rain or the collapse of a man-made structure such as a dam.

hurricane: A severe storm with very high winds and heavy rain.

levee: A bank built alongside water in order to prevent flooding.

monsoon: A seasonal wind that causes an increase in rainfall.

National Weather Service: The official government weather forecasting agency.

stilts: Poles or posts that make something stand off the ground.

INDEX

TO LEARN MORE

Learning more is as easy as 1, 2, 3.

1) Go to www.factsurfer.com
2) Enter "floods" into the search box.
3) Click the "Surf" button to see a list of websites.

With factsurfer, finding more information is just a click away.